BROKEN BUT BEAUTIFUL

UNCONDITIONAL BOND

PRIYA RAWAT

This book is dedicated to someone special who encouraged me to fly toward my dreams; who gave me a love and who made me a free. To my loved ones; for always loving and supporting me. This book is also dedicated to everyone you hate to break; because break always make you...

Contents

FOREWORD

BY PRIYA RAWAT In the writing and illustrating of this book my thought has been to express a comprehensive and concise treatise on the love of heart; It has been made as berief as is consist with relationships and bonds. if u really want to know about broken and beautiful stories,you have to read it. The first thing you'll probably want to feel and visualizng my life ,what ,why, where i live and feel .

Preface

The season was of rain and light dizzle. he was travelling on his way to school when i saw him for that time. the rain on his hir and light moisture on his face was making him even better. till now i had seen him calm, but tody for the first time i saw him talking to his friend while laughung, i kept looking at him, i had started liking him beacause of his calmness, but today it has been a whole month. when i saw him laughing, i went crazy he look handsome. i thin about ,what would be the story of him and me, then the school gate came. i never removed him from my sight. that day i understand one thing that "when love is easily obtained, is not love. it is destiny, because when we gets love also get inner peace". for me, just seeing him once a day was a moment of peace. one day,him talking to me for two hours and smilingat what i said was no less than a dream,buy who knew that this sequence would last only for a few days. because i had only a few days left in school. A lot of changes has been passed but didn't change was the desire which was there that moment and is there even today,time changed,we changed and so did the changes . the city changed a lot, some beautiful moments also passed but the only thing that didn't change was the desire.which was come to see him. i wanted to see her face as soon as i closed my eyes and i could not take my eyes off her face. i felt like getting lost in his scent,it seemed as if her silence was saying something to me. the thumping of heart is audible, heat is emanating from his body. i don't know what i feel and what magic was there in his air that me mad. i felt it either he is with me or he was not around me.The sea son was of rain and light dizzle. he was travelling on his way to school when i saw him for the first time. the rain on his hir and light moisture on his face was making him even better. till now i had seen him calm, but tody for the first time i saw him talking to his friend while laughung, i kept looking at him, i had started liking him beacause of his calmness, but today it has been a whole month. when i saw him laughing, i went crazy he look handsome. i thin about ,what would be the story of him and me, then the school gate came. i never removed him from my sight. that day i understand one thing that "when love is easily obtained, is not love. it is destiny, because when we gets love also get inner peace". for me, just seeing him once a day was a moment of peace. one day,him talking to me for two hours and smilingat what i said was no less than a dream,buy who knew that this sequence would last only for a few days. because i had only a few days left in school. A lot of changes has been passed but didn't change was the desire which was there that moment and is there even today,time changed,we changed and so did the changes .

the city changed a lot, some beautiful moments also passed but the only thing that didn't change was the desire.which was come to see him. i wanted to see her face as soon as i closed my eyes and i could not take my eyes off her face. i felt like getting lost in his scent,it seemed as if her silence was saying something to me. the thumping of heart is audible, heat is emanating from his body. i don't know what i feel and what magic was there in his air that me mad. i felt it either he is with me or he was not around me.

I

DESIRE

When i saw him on the road for the first time. he wearing white shirt that was looking amazing. but two buttons of his shirt were open, my eyes were just stopping on his tight chest but also his sweat on his face was looking mesmerizing. that day, for the first time, i got to know his name "ABHIMANYU". with great difficulty i turned my eyes away from him and controlled myself there but my eyes were just looking at him. that's how i controlled myself and a time came when i had to changed that school. after a few years, a lot of situations changed, cities changed,but nothing changed that was desire, i met many boys in this journey but i haven't seen anyone like him till date. there is a hope in my heart that one day i will get to meet him. when i will get to see him throughout my life. but we did not know that he would come at such a time. our talks would

start like a stranger. conversation should to be normal but it felt as if the heartbeat didn't stop. i didn't know why i felt this way.then one day we met in the market like a stranger. he and me were unware that day . a meeting would take place, but our eyes were not meeting even after eye contact at that moment. it was becoming difficult for me to control myself, my heart was getting beat faster and then took a look at him, his face troubled with sweat seemed to be getting intoxicated,i felt like hugging him right now.

II
OBSESSION

I am sharvari, a simple girl who wears glasses,innocent,quite, but has big dreams. i never knew when those dreams came true. in school, when i was a simple girl who felt happy just by looking at him. i didn't not talk too much to anyone, but one day i just asked him his name, he said to me-abhimanyu, and yours? then from that that day onwards i became obessed with him.it seemed as if i did not know when he made his obession in my dreams. but time passed, so quickly. no one knows this- "sometimes what we want doesn't happen, but sometimes that's happens what we forget after thinking about it for a moment". i started going crazy thinking about him, i felt obession for him. i neither paid attention nor felt like doing anything. i didn't care about anything , only i was started to go crazy thinking about him. aal i felt like doing was to

see him,think about him, adopt his habits in every way. remembering his smile, i started smiling and his face started appearing to me from my dreams to reality. one day we crossed by each other and one day when he shook hands, i felt the warmth of his hands. from that day till today , i have been longing to meet him. i have kept the hope of meeting him in a corner of my heart. that time also came like this we didn't know? when we met in a market. i wanted to see him by raising my lowered eyes, but his eyes were already watching me. our eye contact have to became. then i felt like hugging him right then. but i was stopped myself and took my steps back. thinking wheather he also has the same obession for me or not. when i was about to stop my overthinking. he came in front of me and told me that you have changed a lot. but i was about to stop, he came closly, then my heart started beating fast. i didn't know if, he was really coming towards me. then his smell obessed me. again he said to me now you have beacame even more beautiful and hot too. my eyes only stare him. before i could say anything, i saw that he said bye and left with his friend. i had lost his fragrance to such an extent that i was unable to understand what was happening to me. but there was a warmth in my body when he came close to me. i was smiling to myself and trying to understand what was happening? my heart beats get faster when he come near to me. i felt down a strange feeling and i saw him at night in my dreams.

its like he have became habituated for me.

III
ATTRACTION

Come closure to someone is not the same love. it is important to have a bond with him. that bond which make us feel that he is near us. the same bond i started aving with abhimanyu. sometimes seeing her getting drenched in rain on the road. sometimes thinking of kissing him. it was like seeing heaven to the soul. one night i would get so attached to her that i would start kissed her and dreaming with her. i was get lost in dreams with him. spending time meeting him,talking to him, seeing him, everything seems like a dream. but who knew that with this one i will get lost in dreams with him. time spent, meeting her, talking to her, seeing her, everything seemed like a dream. but who knew that 6-7 years would pass like this. but that desire never ended. that attachement kept growing deeper, but one day , i went to a club for a party of one of my friends.we had

thought of going to a club someday, but i haven't gonr till now. that attachement kept growing deeper. college will be over and job will be started. everyone was dancing in the club, then our firend made me drink something and said take a shot and enjoy vodka. "life is one, then when wil you live it". After hearing this we also became filmy and started enjoying. then a boy came there and asked if we would dance with him and for a moment we decided to refuse but then we remembered our friend tina's words and we danced. after the party when i and my friend tine were leaving. our car damaged, then tina took a lift from the guy with whom i had danced, till now i didn't know his name. meanwhile tina's boyfriend arrives and tina goes with him in his car. vidhyut tells his name and then the car door is opened for me. i didn't understand how can i go without knowing someone with whom i didn't even know. by the way he looks mesmerzing, has a fit and charm body. after all i have to go home, thinking this and sit in the car. i was starting to get attracted to his. i have been thinking about him. accidently, something was happening. the way his eyes were watching me from top to bottom. i was not feeling bad. i started feeling something for him. then vidhyut realized that i had not closed the door properly. vidhyut had to bend down to close the door. my heart started pounding loudly. then, i asked him to stop the car as soon the car stopped. we held eachother tightly and while kissed for a minute. it seemed as if both of us were waiting for this moment. that attachment was very deep. one night, kisses and then that rift without saying anything. may be that journey lasted till there, after that we never met. beacause the next morning i had to come from chandigarh to delhi.

IV

CONVICTION

I was moving ahead in my life with confidence. but no one knows when, where, how and with whom to meet. i have believe in someone's coming in my life with some memorable memories and hopes. somewhere or the other side , even today feeling of pride started to creep up in my memories. i had come to delhi for a job and started staying there too. but my was thinking something else. one day the thundering clouds of rain and then the rain come. what can we all say about the sweet smell of wet soil with the rain. everyone is crazy about this season. we love your own garden for seeing rain drops. that day, seeing abhimanyu getting drenched on the road again in the heavy rain. it felt like promise was being fulfilled with the rain. to seeing his efforts to him from the rain and make his hair wisely. i becoming intoxicated. i thought i should ask

him to come to my room till the rain stops. but, thinking about it,does he stil remember me after 5 years. the rain is getting intense, the lightning strikes felt as if the thunder was getting intense too. my heart was beating fastly. i went downstairs and asked him to come to the room. he came up with smile. his whole clothes were wet. i was started to get intoxicated by the thought of his charm. then abhimanyu asked me about the washroom and i told him by the gesturing , as soon as he came out of the washroom shirtless again i kept looking at him. i was just trying to memorize such a thing with him. right now i stopping my horny thoughts. then, i asked him for coffee. he repiled yes. my gaze was not able to move away form his look. just a coffee cup slippedfrom my hand and broke. after seeing my conciousness he came closure and said both of us will share a cup of coffee. i shook head in yes, as he took a sip wanted to give me the cup. he suddenly, back it up. then, he said to me. i know u love coffee but right now i need it. with the last sip of coffee, i was feeling afraid that this moment too will pass and be gone once again. when will we meet again? abhimanyu asked this to me. i became silent for a minute. because, somewhere the other side i want to stop him and since long time i have been waiting it. then, i repiled to him what should i tell you? a question came to both of them and we both remained silent for a while. then, abhimanyu said my name sharvari and remove the hair from my face. i get feeling *embarrassed, he asked me you don't have trust on me? my mind was saying how should i tell you how much and when does my heart trusted you. but, i had kept quiet on his question. then seeing the rain stop vidyut smile and went to the washroom. he had to come to say me "ok! we will meet again". it was breaking my heart. then, i saw him going. i stopped him by holding his hand from behind and said that" i have a lot of trust on you. but, never got a chance to tell you".*

V
DISCOVERY

A discoverey for something like this. there is a beautiful discovery which no one can understand till the end of life, when and is it found. we get lost in it, the happiness that is found through that search is more beautiful than the world of dreams. After spending that night,i felt as i had dicovered something. that feeling, thesilence of words and fast breathing, some strange movement in the body and touching my body. today my hands were playing with my body. that i had never felt before. it was as if his breaths were coming very close to my ears. and his lips is in dilemma to touch my lips, just we are putting ourselves in the hands of each other. in the meantime, my phone rang when i saw the side of window with my eyes half open. it was already sun rises up. today, it has been a month since we spent tht beautiful night. beacause at that time we

has not been talked to each other in the last moments.that's why we didn't exchange phone numers. when i saw in my phone, i receieved a mail from a publication and i was called for a meeting for book writing. i quickly prepared and left for every path. i felt a lack of pride every moment. i remembered that night how we were drowned in eachother. that is where the story started. when i did feel it? i was thiking so much that i saw a flash of abhimanyu and his presence. its amazing feeling in my inner body. but i didn't know what would happen, that as soon as i got off the metro i heard a voice saying sharavari. when i saw thi abhimanyu coming running from a distance with smile. i just kept looking at him. abhimanyu told me , you didn't give me your number on that day. he hold my hand and say come with me. he brought me to one side and hugged me tightly and said i miss you a lot. he kissed me on my forhead. as soon as, i was about to say something. he took my phone and gave me his number and tell me to call me soon. we'll meet again and left. i also left for my destination, reached the publication office and saw that everyone was there waiting for publication manager. seeing manager coming everyone stood up and i too. but when i saw this mand his son abhimanyu. i was feeling happy in my inner soul. a smile came on his face and i smiling too. but i had a question in my mind as to when would he know? when i am coming. why didn't you tell me. At the end of the meeting i was hiring as the author for writing the book. everyone face was looking shocked as to how this happened. the question arises for everyone was how the freelance writer who came for first time and got this project." it is that answers to some questions are found only, when the right time comes". Abhimanyu asked me to ride with him in the car, i could not refuse but i didn't know that he had come to my room to drop me. after coming to the room i asked him for coffee. he told me with a slight smile. he made coffee. in a minut abhimanyu's driver come and gives a parcel and leaves. abhimanyu told me that, sharavari take this it is for you and asked me to openit. when i opened it, there was a lovely red saree. abhimanyu me to try it on. i could not refuse and went into the room. i was not able to understand, what was going on? who is discover this strange feeling or someone who is breathing faster like his breath? seeing me in saree, abhimanyu's eyes were looking beautiful even more intense for love. it is not impossible to discover love in life, it is possible to discover the thing that mkaes you feel love slowly. just like sharvari spent her time wearing that saree with abhimanyu. considering every moment as hers, who might have come in search of her dreams. someday, every feeling of abhimanyu has to be felt in the heart of sharvari. for bothof them, they trusted eachother and it was their first discovery of love. the moments they spent together, they created them for themselves, no one can take place in these moments. these are their memories, in which there is trust, attachment,desire and discovery of love.

VI

SELFAPEX

*"Sometimes we get lost in someone that we
don't realize ourselves." This is how something
happened with sharvari when she wore that
saree the whole day and went on a long drive
with him. after that abhimanyu left her in her
room and went home, but sharvari didn't take
off her saree. why she didn't know, she lay
down on the bed as soon as .she came and and
started thinking about abhimanyu. while
thinking, she got lost in her sleep and she losing
all her sleep. it seemed to her that abhimanyu
was there. he was opening her saree with love.
her saree into his hands. she have taken a
fantasy for self. sharvari was lost in
intoxication. she felt pride in his hands and
start loving him. she found pride in her
fantasy. opening a sareee and took off all
clothes, lay down on the bed by himself. she
started playing with own body. the fair*

complexion and the amazing figure of her body were seeming good to her today. sometimes she would stretch her legs and lose herself in own fantasy. touching smoothly our own body from top to bottom by own hands and feeling like a apex in own heart. uff she was enjoying it, madness was visible in her eyes and she was getting difficult to control herself after feeling the pride of body. she doing many movements for a selfapex and loved herself so much. after at the peak of pride she found a selfapex fantasy. she proudly gotted from herself and then spent the night. after spending the night, when the eyes were opened in the first light of the morning. she saw the bad condition of the room and also also look nude herself. she remembered all thing about last night, after rememebering it. she shy with smiling. she understood that, " happiness is within ownself, the way of getting it is different for everyone, but love is found in the person who is in front of you and when you find it, you feel more pride and madness."

VII

FORNICATE

"Sometimes the moments spent together are amazing that we never want to forget them". sharvari gets a text message from abhimanyu for an office party. the party was to be held the next evening after that night. sharvari bought a beautiful dress for party and attempt to make oneself look sexy in front of him. today was the evening when sharvari was getting ready for the party and then another message came that abhimanyu said the he is sending a car to pick her. her happines has made her more excited. she have been blessed with the moon light. she was thinking of kissing abhimanyu today. then she heard doorbell rings and then she sits in the car and leaves for a party. she raches the party thinking about abhimanyu, but when she goes there. she sees that abhimanyu is hugging a girl. sharvari didn't know that girl, actually she only knew that he is the boss of that

company and he is the boy with whom she had crush on him in childhood. sharvari was deeply hurt seeing he hugged some other girl. she wanted to leave the party at the time. when he stopped her and started introducing her to everyone. he started telling that the special person for whom this party has been kept today is sharvari goyenka. she is a very good writer, who will now work with us and move our company with all of us. after that abhimanyu asked her to dance with him. sharvari could not say no and he did a romantic dance with sharvari. everyone started enjoying the party and everyone was lost in themselves and in each other. in such a situation, he takes sharvari to a room where he planned a surprise for her. he had planned a surprise private date. she would be very happy seeing all this. by losing her happiness, she takes all her pride in her heart and hugging him tighlt. both of them embrace each other and get lost for a while. the his phone rings and his friend is calling him to a party. he tells his friend kartik that he has gone away from there. because he had to stay with sharvari. they have dinner and talk a lot. both of them drink alchol heavily too. by listening to each other's talks they know each other since childhood . he hugs her while kissing her. she also kisses wildely him while holding his head. both of them started feeling lost in each other. he kissed her on her neck wildely. he touched her body here and there. she felt loosing herself in his hands. she was also *opened the buttons of his shirt. he was kissing her amazing body from top to bottom and she was feeling love by feeling his kiss with her closed eyes. she being kissed him, sometimes from the front and from the back. she seduced him widely. they touched each other's body in such a way that even feeling of selfapex,immersed in each other. they love each other a lot even today. the whole body of pride is caressed by the soft hands of the soul when he touched her breast tightly with love. then hearing she sounds aaaahh. he loved her even more and more. seeing she felt so intoxicated. they started loving widely and kissed so hardly. after listening to she is so sexy voice and getting his love. both are unable to control each other. while doing kissed and hard fornicate. for a moment both of them feeling intoxicated while loving each other. perhaps, neither of them has experienced that fantasy before. after getting lost in deep love. next morning brings new begining. the last night that both of them spent together under influence of alchol, hardly anyone will never forget. they reached home as soon as morning arrived. both of them were thinking whether whatever happened was right.*

VIII
RIFT

" Sometimes a few moments are enough to seperate from each other . even when we are seperated due to paths, the distance ends. but if there is a crack in the heart. it takes time to heal. and when it will happen is also not known, or wheather it will happen or not, nothing is known. something similar happened with sharvari, when she saw him kissing someone in his cabin while fixing her hair. sharvari too was heartbroken, she started thinking that he was doing with her last night was it a joke? is she a stupid girl? when abhimanyu saw sharvari, he suddenly came to sharvari and told her that it is not as you are thinking. today, sharvari was only feeling angry and lonely at herself. beacause the boy for whom she had been waiting till now was not at all as she was thinking. she immediately leaves the office and seeing abhimanyu worried *behind leaving her. the office people wonder what would have happened that the boss is so worried for sharvari.there is a notification sound on everyone's phone. everyone gets shocked seeing the news on their phones together that sharvari has left the book project and rejected the whole agreements. coninue abhimanyu kept on messaging and calls her, sometimes he even visuted her house but sharvari was not there. Sometimes one of our mistakes creates a rift in the relationships.and sometimes even the truth which we have heard can be rejected for oce but whatever we see with our eyes. we keep it in our mind and even trying to forget it, but we are not able to forget it. "Nobody comes empty handed into our life.they bring their past along. they bring along their pain,nervousness,their struggles,their memories,their scratches and marks. they bring along everything". never get confused and lose out on each other.*

www.ingramcontent.com/pod-product-compliance
Lightning Source LLC
Chambersburg PA
CBHW051420130726
47989CB00007B/3006